WALL PILATES WORKOUT

Aaron Wright

WALL PILATES WORKOUT

Illustrated Easy Exercises Guide for Women, Seniors & Beginners, No Equipment, to Achieve Strength, Stretching, Balance, Flexibility, Lose Weight

TABLE OF CONTENTS

INTRODUCTION

Congratulations on taking the big, bold step to try out this book. Wall Pilates Workout is a carefully curated collection of 100 simple, practical, and effective Wall Pilates exercises that will help you achieve a measurable transformation in your health and overall wellness.

Ideally, Wall Pilates is a unique variation of basic Pilates exercises that incorporates the support of a wall and the simplicity of a mat to provide holistic health benefits. The exercises in this book include poses like pressing your feet, arms, back, and sides against a wall, all working together to enhance your strength, balance, flexibility, posture, and overall coordination.

Are you a senior interested in defying the norms of aging, a woman seeking to lose weight, or someone who just wants to stay in shape? The contents of this book are all you need to stay fit and appear agile at all times, with just a mat and a favorite corner in your space.

These exercises are beginner-friendly and can be performed by anyone anywhere, irrespective of age or experience level, making it a great companion you should consider for your next vacation. Also, with the extra pages containing a workout plan, TUDCA and its benefits, and other recommendations provided at the end of this book, all you need is consistency and commitment to witness your journey toward flexibility, agility, and resistance!

CORE BUILDING EXERCISES

1. WALL-POWERED PLANK REACH

Difficulty: Intermediate

Duration: 5 minutes

Repetitions: 3 sets x 10 reps (per arm)

Instructions:

1. Stand 2 feet from the wall.

2. Feet hip-width apart.

3. Lean forward, hands on the wall shoulder-width apart.

4. Keep a slanted line from heels to head, engaging core.

5. Lift your right hand, reaching up without rotating your torso.

6. Return hand to the wall and repeat with left arm.

7. Exhale when reaching, inhale when returning your hand to the wall.

2. CORE-STRENGTHENING WALL SQUAT

Difficulty: Intermediate

Duration: 8 minutes

Repetitions: 3 sets x 15 reps

Instructions:

1. Stand with your back against the wall, feet shoulder-width apart.
2. Descend into a squat, keeping thighs parallel to the floor.
3. Engage core throughout.
4. Press down on your heels to return to the initial position.

3. STANDING WALL TWISTS

Difficulty: Beginner

Duration: 5 Minutes

Sets and Reps: 3 sets x 10 twists (per side)

Instructions:

1. Stand facing the wall with your right side, feet hip-width apart.

2. Bend your arms at shoulder height, palms forward, and lightly touch the wall with your right hand.

3. Rotate your torso to the left, letting your right hand glide along the wall.

4. Feel the stretch in your side muscles, hold briefly, then return to the starting position.

5. Switch sides and repeat.

6. Keep your hips and feet facing forward, and engage your core.

4. ISOMETRIC WALL PLANK HOLD

Difficulty: Intermediate

Duration: 5 Minutes

Sets and Reps: 3 sets x 60 seconds hold

Instructions:

1. Stand approximately 2 feet away from a wall, facing it.
2. Position your hands flat on the wall, shoulder-width apart, and step your feet back to create a slanted plank.
3. Engage your core and maintain a straight body line.
4. Hold the position, concentrating on even breathing.

5. VERTICAL WALL SIT & TWIST

Difficulty: Intermediate

Duration: 8 Minutes

Sets and Reps: 5 sets x 4 reps (right and left twists count as one rep)

Instructions:

1. Stand 2 feet away from the wall, with your back against it, descending into a wall sit position.

2. Extend your arms forward, twist your torso to the right, then return to the center.

3. Repeat the twist on the left side.

4. Ensure your hips and lower body remain stationary during the twists.

6. WALL SQUAT HOLDS

Difficulty: Beginner

Duration: 6 Minutes

Sets and Reps: 5 sets x 60 seconds holds

Instructions:

1. Position yourself with your back against the wall, placing your feet 2 feet (60 cm) away, shoulder-width apart.

2. Slide down the wall, bending your knees to create a right angle, and aligning your knees over your ankles.

3. Press your lower back against the wall, keeping your shoulders relaxed, and place your hands at your sides or on your thighs.

4. Engage your core and glutes to maintain the squat position.

7. WALL-TOUCH FORWARD BEND WITH PULSA-TIONS

Difficulty: Intermediate

Sets and Reps: Not applicable

Instructions:

1. Stand facing the wall.
2. Hinge forward from your hips until your upper body is parallel to the ground.
3. Extend your arms and press your palms against the wall.
4. While maintaining pressure against the wall, gently pulse your upper body downward for 20-30 seconds, focusing on stretching your back and hamstrings.

8. WALL CRISS CROSS

Difficulty: Moderate

Duration: 14 repetitions (7 on each side)

Instructions:

1. Lie on your back, hands behind your head, legs at a 45-degree angle.
2. Lift head, neck, and shoulders.
3. Rotate the left armpit towards the right knee, bringing the right knee in.
4. Release and rotate to the opposite side.
5. Continue for 14 reps.

9. WALL DEAD BUG

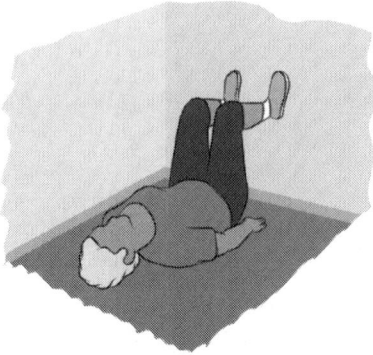

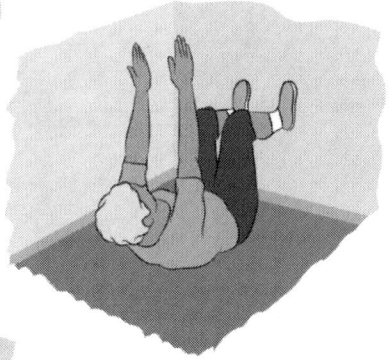

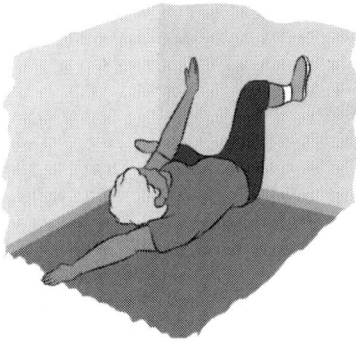

Difficulty: Intermediate

Duration: 10 Minutes

Sets and Reps: 3 sets x 12 reps (on each side)

Instructions:

1. Lie on your back, with your legs against the wall, forming a 90-degree angle.

2. Flatten your lower back against the mat.

3. Extend one leg while lowering the opposite arm.

4. Gently return to the initial position.

5. Alternate sides.

10. WALL DEAD BUG WITH ARM SLIDE

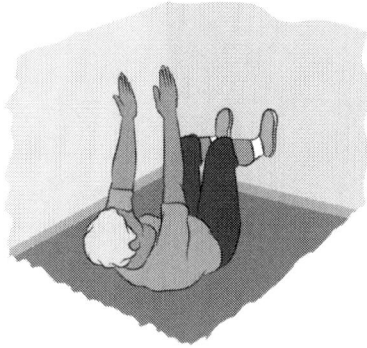

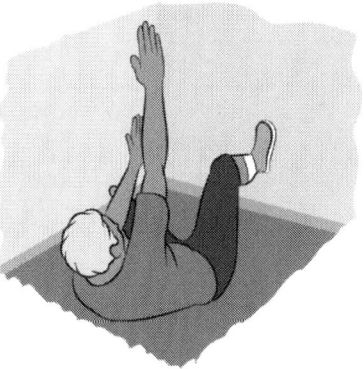

Difficulty: Intermediate

Duration: 11 Minutes

Sets and Reps: 3 sets x 12 reps (on each side)

Instructions:

1. Lie on your back, legs against the wall, with your arms straight up.
2. Slide one hand upwards while extending the opposite leg.
3. Return to the starting position.
4. Alternate sides.

11. WALL PUSH-UPS

Difficulty: Beginner

Duration: 7 Minutes

Sets and Reps: 3 sets x 15 reps

Instructions:

1. Stand facing a wall, approximately 2 feet away, with hands flat on the wall, slightly wider than shoulder-width apart.

2. Activate core muscles and maintain a straight alignment from head to heels.

3. Flex your elbows and lean toward the wall until your nose is close to it.

4. Exhale, and extend arms to return to the initial position.

12. ISOMETRIC WALL PRESS

Difficulty: Beginner

Duration: 5 Minutes

Sets and Press: 4 sets x 20 seconds press

Instructions:

1. Stand facing a sturdy wall, placing your hands on the wall a bit beyond shoulder width.

2. Spread fingers wide, engage the core, and press into the wall without visible movement.

3. Hold the press, maintaining a tight core and controlled breathing.

13. WALL-SUPPORTED PLANK TO PIKE

Difficulty: Intermediate

Duration: 9 Minutes

Sets and Reps: 4 sets x 10 reps

Instructions:

1. Place the exercise mat perpendicular to the wall.

2. Get into a plank position with your feet close to the wall.

3. Inhale, push feet up the wall, lifting hips into a pike position.

4. Exhale, lower back to the plank position.

14. WALL PLANK

Difficulty: Beginner

Duration: 20-30 seconds (gradually extend)

Reps and Set: Repeat as desired

Instructions:

1. Place your hands and forearms flat against the wall, slightly wider than shoulder-width apart.
2. Walk your feet back and lean into the wall, creating a straight line from head to heels.
3. Uphold the plank position, keeping your core engaged.
4. Inhale and exhale steadily, avoiding breath retention.
5. Gradually elongate the duration over time.

15. WALL ROLL-DOWNS

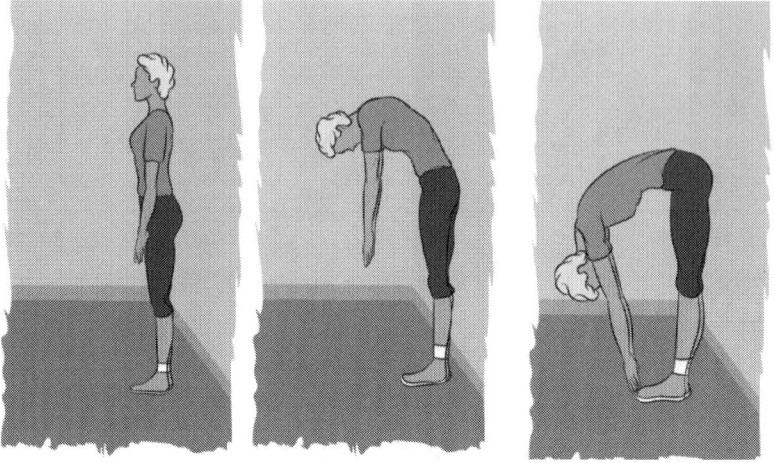

Difficulty: Easy

Duration: Repeat 5 times

Instructions:

1. Stand with your back against the wall, arms comfortably lowered on each side.

2. Ensure your feet are a few inches away from the wall.

3. Tuck your chin to your chest.

4. Begin to roll down slowly, lowering your hands to the mat and allowing your back to round.

5. Bend your knees if necessary.

6. Pause at the bottom, with the crown of your head pointing toward the floor.

7. Roll back up, restacking the spine, and lifting your head last.

8. Repeat the sequence five times.

16. WALL PLANK WITH BACK KICK

Difficulty: Moderate

Duration: Repeat 3 times per leg

Instructions:

1. Face the wall, standing a few feet away.
2. Extend your arms and lean your palms and forearms against the wall, shoulder-width apart.
3. Engage your core, ensuring a straight line from head to heels.
4. Move your left leg backward while maintaining the upper body plank position.
5. Lift your leg as high as possible.
6. Return the leg down.
7. Repeat the sequence three times.
8. Perform the same sequence with the right leg.
9. To exit, place both feet on the ground and walk toward the wall.

17. WALL TEASER

Difficulty: Advanced

Duration: Execute 10 repetitions

Reps and Set: Repeat as desired

Instructions:

1. Initiate by reclining, with feet directed toward the wall.
2. Position your feet against the wall and elevate your arms over your head.
3. Activate your core, elevate your head akin to a sit-up, and extend your hands toward the wall.
4. Return to the initial position and repeat for 10 reps.

18. WALL OBLIQUE CRUNCHES

Difficulty: Intermediate

Duration: 10 Minutes

Sets and Reps: 3 sets x 12 reps (6 on each side)

Instructions:

1. Stand sideways to the wall, with the left side closest.
2. Position your feet hip-width apart, with your left hand on the wall.
3. Tighten your core, and raise your right knee toward your left elbow.
4. Inhale as you return to the starting position.
5. Switch sides and repeat.

19. STRAIGHT LEGGED SIT UPS

Difficulty: Intermediate

Duration: Repeat for 10 iterations

Reps and Set: Repeat as desired

Instructions:

1. Lie on your back with legs straight up against the wall and feet together.

2. Activate your core, lift your head off the ground, and ascend your hands upward, initiating from your core.

3. Gradually lower back down to the starting position and repeat for 10 iterations.

20. WALL ASSISTED HALF BODY PLANK

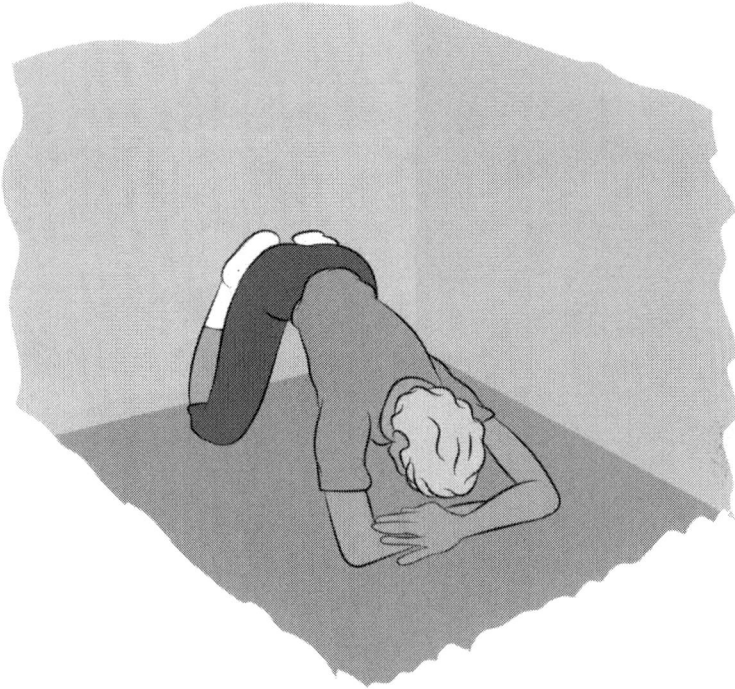

Difficulty: Intermediate

Duration: Perform 8-10 repetitions

Reps and Set: Repeat as desired

Instructions:

1. Commence in a kneeling posture, shift backward, and elongate your legs up the wall into a downward dog.

2. Gradually advance forward into a plank position, up-holding head alignment and focusing on the ground.

3. Repeat for 8-10 reps, emphasizing breath regulation and shoulder steadiness.

21. WALL ROLL UP

Difficulty: Intermediate

Duration: Execute poses 4 times

Reps and Set: Repeat as desired

Instructions:

1. Recline with your entire body weight resting on the floor.

2. Extend your arms straight backward with toes braced against the wall for resistance.

3. Inhale, lifting arms straight up with toes pointed upward.

4. Exhale, slowly lowering your chin and head forward.

5. While exhaling, roll forward to your comfort level and
    sustain for 10 seconds.

6. Repeat the poses 4 times, utilizing breath for movement
    guidance.

22. ROTATING PLANKS

Difficulty: Moderate

Duration: 10 repetitions (5 on each side)

Instructions:

1. Start in a standard plank position, arms straight, and body in a straight line.

2. Engage the core, shift weight left, and rotate upward to a side plank on the right.

3. Hold briefly, and return to plank.

4. Rotate right, lifting left arm into the sky for a left side plank.

5. Continue alternating sides for 10 repetitions

23. WALL HUNDREDS

Difficulty: Moderate

Duration: Pump for 100 counts

Instructions:

1. Lie on your back, with legs at a 45-degree angle and feet against the wall.

2. Lift your head, neck, and shoulders, extending arms by your sides, palms facing down.

3. Pump your arms up and down in small, controlled movements.

4. Inhale for 5 pumps, exhale for 5 pumps.

5. Try for 100 pumps, or incrementally (20, 40, 60, 80, 100).

6. After pumps, relax the head, neck, shoulders, and legs on the floor.

24. SINGLE-LEG PUSH-OFF

Difficulty: Intermediate

Duration: 10 Minutes

Sets and Reps: 10 sets x 3 reps (per leg)

Instructions:

1. Stand two feet away from the wall, directly facing it.
2. Place your hands on the wall slightly wider than shoulder-width apart.
3. Shift your balance to your right foot, lifting your left foot.
4. Engage your core, keeping your back straight.
5. Bend your elbows, and lean your torso toward the wall.

6. Push yourself away from the wall by straightening your arms.

7. Complete the required reps before switching legs.

8. Maintain control, using your chest and arm muscles for the push-off.

BALANCE EXERCISES

25. ELEVATED STALLION PULSES

Difficulty: Intermediate

Duration: 8 Minutes

Sets and Pulses: 4 sets x 15 pulses (each side)

Instructions:

1. Begin on hands and knees, lifting your knees slightly above the mat.

2. Raise one foot toward the ceiling and pulse up and down.

3. Switch legs after completing the repetitions.

26. STANDING WALL SINGLE-LEG BALANCE

Difficulty: Beginner

Duration: 6 Minutes

Sets and Reps: 3 sets x 30 seconds per leg

Instructions:

1. Stand with your back to the wall, maintaining a distance of 1 foot.
2. Lift one leg, bending the knee to a 90-degree angle.
3. Extend your arms for balance or lightly press your hands against the wall.
4. Engage your core and uphold a straight posture.
5. Maintain the single-leg stance.

27. WALL-SUPPORTED TREE POSE STRETCH

Difficulty: Beginner

Duration: 5 Minutes

Sets and Reps: 3 sets x 30 seconds per side

Instructions:

1. Stand sideways, 2 feet away from the wall.
2. Ground your left foot, raising your right foot against the inner left calf or thigh.
3. Utilize the wall for support, placing your hands on the wall or in a prayer position.
4. Hold the stretch and maintain balance.
5. Switch sides and repeat.

28. WALL MARCHES

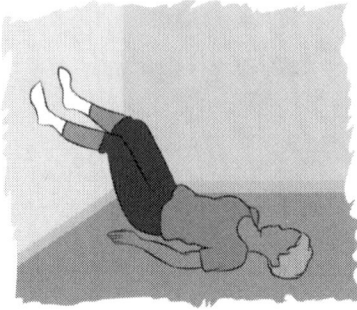

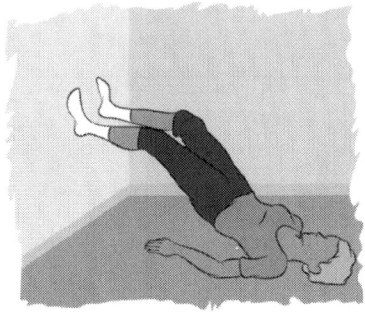

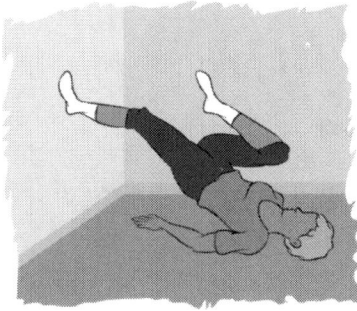

Difficulty: Beginner

Duration: As required

Lifts: 8-10 raises per leg

Instructions:

1. Position both feet against the wall while lying flat.

2. Propel off the wall until your buttocks point upward, steadying your arched back with your arms on the ground.

3. Gradually lift your right leg toward your chest, maintaining pelvic stability.

4. Lower the right foot back to the wall and repeat with the left leg.

5. Strive for 8-10 lifts with each leg, concentrating on preserving pelvic stability.

29. CONTROL BALANCE

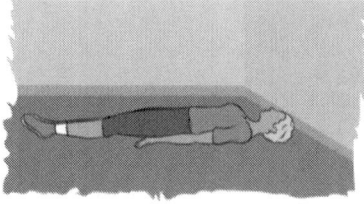

Difficulty: Intermediate

Duration: Perform 6 total leg switches

Reps and Set: Repeat as desired

Instructions:

1. Initiate lying on your back with your feet pointing away from the wall.

2. Elevate your legs, grasping your feet (or ankles) with your hands, employing the wall for stability if required.

3. Hoist one leg straight up, switch leg positions, and replicate 3 times per leg (6 total).

4. Utilize the wall for assistance if necessary, emphasizing deliberate, measured movements.

30. WALL DOWNWARD DOG

Difficulty: Beginner

Duration: Hold for 15 seconds

Reps and Set: Repeat as desired

Instructions:

1. Initiate with your back against the wall, lean forward, touching the ground with your hands.

2. Gradually progress your hands forward, utilizing the wall for support against your feet.

3. Extend your back upward and backward to your comfort level, sustaining for 15 seconds.

4. Inhale as you advance forward, and exhale as you press into your feet.

31. HIGH LUNGE POSE

Difficulty: Beginner

Duration: Sustain for 3 breaths

Reps and Set: Repeat 3 times per leg (6 total)

Instructions:

1. Initiate from a standing stance facing the wall.

2. Extend one foot backward as far as possible, with the heel slightly raised.

3. Slightly flex the knee on the opposing leg and position your hands against the wall.

4. Extend and raise your head upward and backward, sustaining for 3 breaths.

5. Reverse leg positions and repeat 3 times for a total of 6 reps.

32. WALL SIDE PLANK

Difficulty: Intermediate

Duration: Hold for 10 seconds per side

Reps and Set: Repeat 2 times per side

Instructions:

1. Position yourself sideways about an arm's length from a wall, extending the arm closest to the wall.

2. Rest your hand on the wall at a comfortable height, with the other hand on your waist.

3. Align your feet together, shifting weight onto the foot closest to the wall, maintaining for 10 seconds.

4. Alternate sides and repeat for 10 seconds, completing 2 rounds per side.

33. SUPPORTED WARRIOR 3

Difficulty: Intermediate

Duration: Hold for several breaths

Reps and Set: Repeat as desired

Instructions:

1. Lean over facing the wall, placing hands on it with arms extended.

2. Transfer weight onto one foot, gradually raising the opposite leg while maintaining a straight back.

3. Lean your upper body forward towards the ground until a straight line is achieved.

4. Maintain the position for several breaths, then return to standing, and repeat on the other side.

34. PUPPY DOG WALL POSE

Difficulty: Easy

Duration: Hold for 30 seconds to 1 minute per iteration

Instructions:

1. Begin by kneeling about an arm's length away from a wall.

2. Extend arms forward and place palms flat against the wall.

3. Lift your hips and extend your arms upward, allowing your head to naturally rise.

4. Deepen the stretch by gently pressing your palms into the wall and sinking your chest towards it.

5. To release, lower your hips onto your legs.

35. LEGS UP THE WALL POSE

Difficulty: Easy

Duration: Hold for 30 seconds

Instructions:

1. Position your mat perpendicular to a wall, with one hip touching it.

2. Swing your legs up onto the wall as you lie back on the mat, ensuring your buttocks are close to or touching the wall.

3. Place arms at your sides, palms facing up.

4. Relax and breathe deeply, maintaining the pose for 30 seconds.

5. To exit, bend your knees, roll to one side, and gently push up to a seated position.

36. WALL SHOULDER STAND

Difficulty: Moderate

Duration: Maintain position for 20-30 seconds

Instructions:

1. Position your mat perpendicular to a wall, lying down with your feet facing it.

"Just in case I fall" version:

2. Swing your feet upward in the air as you bring your hands to your back to steady your legs.

3. Press your hands into your waist and extend both legs straight up.

Wall Assist Version:

4. Bring your legs up onto the wall, adjusting so your buttocks are close to or touching the wall.

5. Press your hands into your waist and walk both legs straight up the wall.

6. See if you can move your legs away from the wall while maintaining balance.

7. To exit, bend your knees, slowly lower your spine down, and roll to one side.

37. WALL HALF HAPPY BABY POSE

Difficulty: Easy

Duration: Hold for a few seconds (5 deep breaths)

Instructions:

1. Lie on your back close to a wall with your legs extended up it.
2. With legs extended straight up the wall, bend one knee towards your chest.
3. Hold the outer edge of the foot of the bent leg, gently pressing the knee towards the floor beside your torso.
4. Relax and breathe, holding for a few seconds.
5. Switch and repeat with the other leg.

38. WALL HANDSTAND

Difficulty: Moderate to Advanced

Duration: Hold for 3 breaths

Instructions:

1. Find a sturdy wall with ample space.

2. Stand facing the wall with 2 feet of space between your foot and the wall.

3. Place hands on the floor shoulder-width apart, about 1 foot from the wall.

4. Kick up into a handstand, bringing both feet against the wall.

5. Stack hips over shoulders and shoulders over wrists.

6. Keep fingers spread wide, pressing palms into the ground.

7. Engage core and legs, pointing toes towards the ceiling.

8. Hold the position, inhale, and exhale for 3 breaths.

9. Carefully kick forward and descend 1 leg at a time.

39. WALL HANDSTAND LEG EXTENSIONS

Difficulty: Moderate to Advanced

Duration: 3 slow reps on each leg

Instructions:

1. Find a sturdy wall with ample space.

2. Stand facing it with 2-3 feet of space.

3. Place hands on the floor about shoulder-width apart, 1-5 feet away from the wall.

4. Kick up into a handstand, aligning hips over shoulders and shoulders over wrists.

5. Spread fingers wide, press palms into the ground, engage the core, and maintain a straight back.

6. Slowly bend your left knee, keeping the other leg pointing up.

7. Hold for 5 seconds, then raise the leg back up.

8. Repeat the knee bend with the right leg for 3 slow reps each, totaling 6.

9. Carefully exit the handstand by cartwheeling or pushing your feet off the wall.

10. Rest and shake out your wrists.

FLEXIBILITY EXERCISES

40. STANDING SIDE BEND POSE

Difficulty: Easy

Duration: Hold for a few breaths

Instructions:

1. Stand sideways about an arm's length from a wall with feet firmly planted and close together.

2. Extend the arm furthest from the wall overhead and place that hand on the wall for support.

3. Take a deep breath in, and exhale as you gently bend your torso for a deep stretch.

4. Simultaneously, extend the opposite arm alongside and down your body for an additional stretch.

5. Hold for a few breaths, feeling the stretch along your sides.

6. Switch sides

7. Turn around and repeat on the opposite side, performing 3 stretches per side for about 15 seconds each.

41. WALL-ASSISTED LEG CIRCLES

Difficulty: Intermediate

Duration: 6 minutes

Repetitions: 3 sets x 10 circles (each leg)

Instructions:

1. Lie flat on a mat with feet against the wall, forming a right angle at the knees.
2. Keep hips 18 inches away from the wall.
3. Straighten your right leg towards the ceiling, pointing your toes.
4. Perform controlled circular movements with your right foot.
5. Switch to the left leg, keeping the core engaged and maintaining a neutral spine.

42. WALL-SUPPORTED PISTOL SQUATS

Difficulty: Intermediate

Duration: 7 Minutes

Sets and Reps: 4 sets x 5 reps (for each leg)

Instructions:

1. Stand with your back to the wall, 1 foot away, with your feet shoulder-width apart.

2. Raise your right leg straight ahead, balancing on your left foot.

3. Gradually lower into a deep squat on your left leg, utilizing the wall for support.

4. Push through your left heel to return to the starting position.

5. Repeat the process with the opposite leg.

43. TWISTED LEG STRETCH

Difficulty: Intermediate
Duration: 5 Minutes
Instructions:
1. Lie on a comfortable surface or mat with your back on the floor.
2. Place your feet against the wall at a 45-degree angle
3. Breathe in as you use your toes to turn both legs to the right, creating a twist.
4. Hold this twist for five seconds as you exhale
5. Revert to starting position and repeat the movement on the left side for another five seconds.
6. Do the left and right movement five times on each side to make ten repetitions.

44. CHILD'S POSE

Difficulty: Beginner

Duration: Up to a minute

Repetitions: Repeat as desired

Instructions:

1. Begin in a tabletop position with your wrists under your shoulders and your knees under your hips.

2. Push your hips back toward your heels, lowering your torso between your thighs.

3. Stretch your arms out in front, palms facing down on the floor.

4. Bring your forehead to the ground.

5. Stay in this pose for up to a minute.

45. HAPPY BABY

Difficulty: Beginner

Duration: 30 seconds to a few minutes

Repetitions: Repeat as desired

Instructions:

1. Lying on the floor, bend your knees and bring them towards your chest.

2. Reach up to grab the outer edges of your knees with your hands.

3. If it feels good, gently rock from side to side or up and down.

4. Stay in this pose for anywhere from 30 seconds to a few minutes.

5. To come out of the pose, gently release your feet and lay them down on the mat.

46. THUNDERBOLT POSE

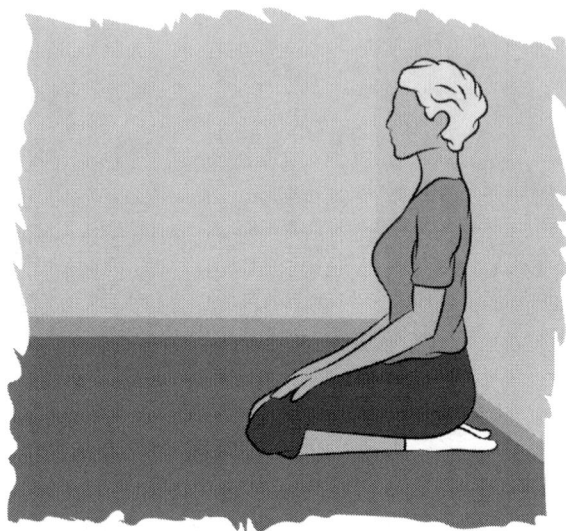

Difficulty: Beginner

Duration: Hold as needed

Repetitions: Repeat as desired

Instructions:

1. Start by kneeling on the floor or a yoga mat with feet together.
2. Sit back so that your buttocks are resting on your heels.
3. Ensure your spine is straight and erect.
4. Place your hands on your thighs, palms facing down.
5. Drop your shoulders down and away from your ears.
6. Keep your head straight, with your gaze directed forward.

47. STRADDLE POSE

Difficulty: Easy

Duration: Hold for as long as comfortable

Instructions:

1. Position your mat perpendicular to a wall, sitting sideways against it.

2. Swing your legs up onto the wall as you lie back on the mat, ensuring your buttocks are close to or touching the wall.

3. Extend your legs straight up the wall.

4. Gradually open your legs into a "V" shape, allowing gravity to pull them towards the floor.

5. Relax your arms straight down each side.

6. Breathe deeply and relax, maintaining the pose for as long as comfortable.

7. To exit, gently use your hands to assist in bringing your legs back together, then bend your knees and roll to one side.

48. QUAD STRETCH WITH WALL SUPPORT

Difficulty: Intermediate

Sets and Reps: Not applicable

Instructions:

1. Face the wall and place both hands against it.
2. Bend one knee, bringing the heel towards your glutes.
3. Hold your ankle with the hand on the same side.
4. Maintain the stretch for 20-30 seconds before switching to the other leg.

49. WALL COW POSE

Difficulty: Easy

Duration: Not specified

Repetitions: 5 relaxing cycles

Instructions:

1. Commence on all fours with your toes against the wall for added stability.

2. Inhale, arch your spine by dropping your belly towards the mat and lifting your head and tailbone towards the ceiling.

3. Exhale, maintaining the arched position for 3 seconds.

4. Repeat for 5 soothing cycles.

50. HALF PLOUGH POSE

Difficulty: Moderate

Duration: Hold for a few seconds (5 breaths)

Instructions:

1. Lie down with legs facing away from the wall and head a few inches away.

2. Slowly kick your legs upward and backward until reaching the wall.

3. Ensure legs are parallel to the floor and toes point downward.

4. Lay arms sideways on the floor or use them for stabilization by placing them beside the core.

5. Breathe deeply and hold for a few seconds (about 5 breaths).

6. To exit, bend your legs and slowly roll to the side or swing your legs back to a neutral laying position.

51. CORPSE POSE

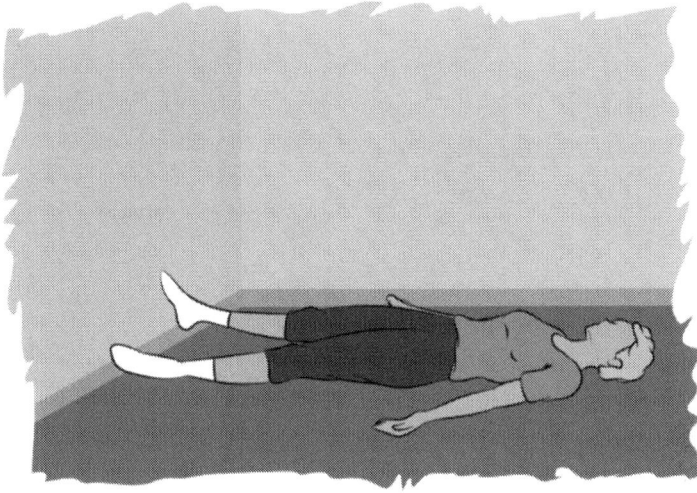

Difficulty: Beginner

Duration: Up to 60 seconds (or up to 5 minutes after a full workout routine)

Repetitions: Repeat as desired

Instructions:

1. Begin by lying flat on your back on a yoga mat or a soft surface.
2. Let your feet fall open naturally, positioning them approximately hip-width apart or wider.
3. Place your arms alongside your body, palms facing upwards.
4. Release any tension from the body and let your muscles soften.
5. Stay in this position for up to 60 seconds.

52. WALL BRIDGE EXTENSIONS

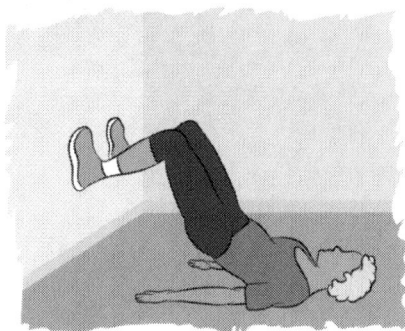

Difficulty: Intermediate

Duration: 8 Minutes

Sets and Reps: 3 sets x 10 reps (5 reps per leg)

Instructions:

1. Lie on your back with feet against the wall, and knees forming a 90-degree angle.
2. Lift your hips and push your feet against the wall.
3. Extend one leg straight while keeping the other foot pressing into the wall.
4. Hold the leg extension, return the foot to the wall, and lower your hips.
5. Repeat the process with the opposite leg.

53. WALL-SUPPORTED SINGLE-LEG SQUATS

Difficulty: Intermediate

Duration: 6 Minutes

Sets and Reps: 3 sets x 12 reps (per leg)

Instructions:

1. Stand with your back against the wall, keeping your feet 2 feet away.

2. Lean back slightly, ensuring your upper back is against the wall.

3. Lift your right knee and perform a single-leg squat with your left leg.

4. Engage your core, maintain an erect spine, and control the motion.

5. Lower your right leg and switch to the left leg.

54. WALL SPLIT PROGRESSIONS

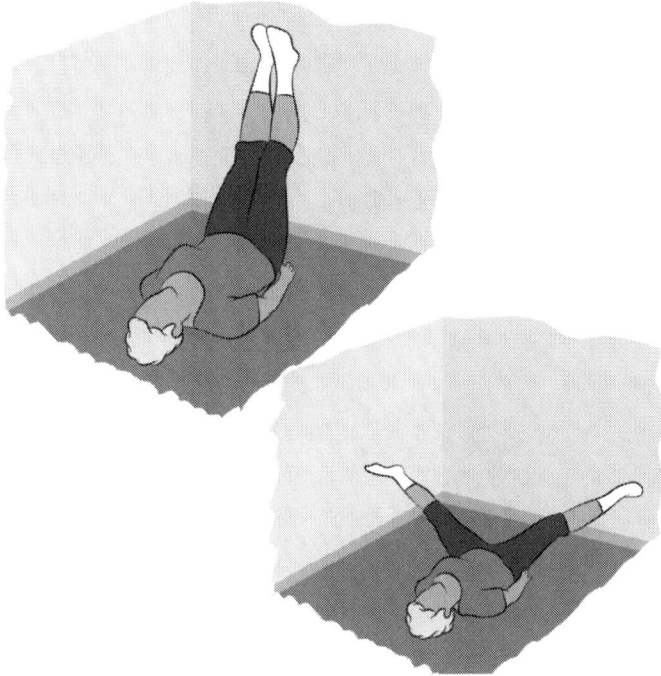

Difficulty: Intermediate

Duration: 8 Minutes

Sets and Reps: 3 sets x 15 reps

Instructions:

1. Lie down with your buttocks close to the wall, extending your legs straight up.

2. Open your legs to the sides, pressing them against the wall.

3. Maintain the stretch, allowing gravity to aid in widening the legs.

4. Utilize your hands to guide the legs back to the center and gently lower them down.

55. FORWARD FOLD AGAINST WALL

Difficulty: Easy

Duration: Hold for up to 30 seconds

Instructions:

1. Stand a few feet away from the wall, facing it.

2. Ensure your feet are hip-width apart and parallel.

3. Lean forward, lowering your head until your hands or upper body make contact with the wall.

4. Press your hips back to intensify the stretch in your hamstrings and lower back.

5. Breathe deeply, holding the position for up to 30 seconds.

6. To exit, press into your feet, lift your torso and return to a standing position.

56. STANDING BACKBEND POSE

Difficulty: Moderate

Duration: Hold for up to 30 seconds

Instructions:

1. Stand facing the wall, position yourself about a foot or two away, and adjust based on your flexibility.
2. Keep your feet comfortably apart.
3. Lean back, placing your hands on the wall behind you with your fingers pointing down.
4. Press into your feet, engaging your thighs and core.

5. Lift your chest upward, arching your back, and if comfortable, let your head gently drop backward.

6. Use the wall for support by pushing against it with your hands.

7. Breathe deeply, maintaining the pose for up to 30 seconds.

8. To exit, engage your core, slowly lift your torso, and return to a neutral standing position.

57. GARLAND POSE WITH WALL

Difficulty: Easy

Duration: Hold for up to 30 seconds

Instructions:

1. Stand with back against a wall, feet wider than hip-width apart, toes turned slightly out.
2. Squat down, aiming to keep heels grounded.
3. Allow thighs to be wider than the torso, pressing elbows against inner knees.
4. Join palms together in front of your chest.
5. Gently press hips and lower back against the wall for alignment and support.
6. Breathe deeply, holding for up to 30 seconds.
7. Release by pressing onto feet and returning to standing position.

58. WALL-ASSISTED NECK STRETCHES

Difficulty: Beginner

Sets/Reps: 2/10-15 (each side)

Time: 3 Minutes

Instructions:

1. Stand facing the wall with feet shoulder-width apart.
2. Place your right hand on the wall for stability.
3. Tilt your head to the left, feeling a gentle stretch along the right side of your neck.
4. Hold for a few seconds and return to the starting position.
5. Repeat on the opposite side.
6. Perform 10-15 stretches on each side.

59. SCAPULA STRETCH

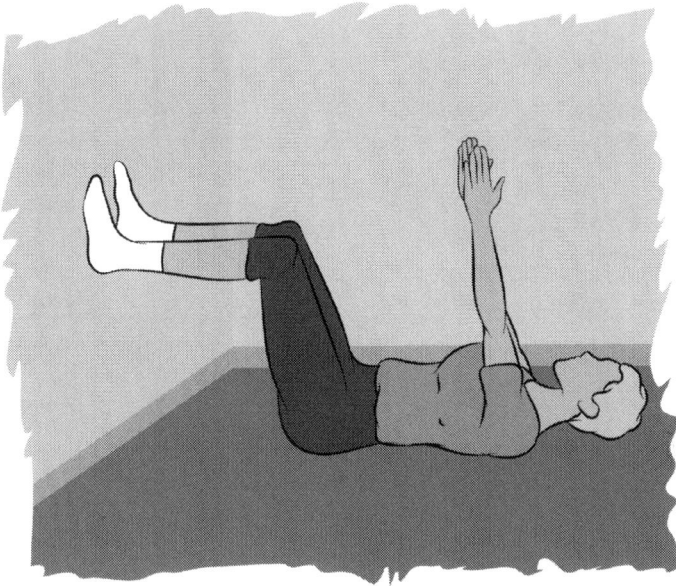

Difficulty: Beginner

Duration: Not specified

Sets and Reps: 10 repetitions

Instructions:

1. Lie on your back with your foot against the wall at a 90-degree angle.

2. Inhale, extend your hands upward, grasp for 2 seconds.

3. Exhale, and release hands back to the original position.

4. Repeat for 10 repetitions.

60. WALL LEG STRETCH

Difficulty: Intermediate

Duration: 30 seconds on each side

Sets and Reps: 1 set on each side

Instructions:

1. Position your right foot against the wall and bend your left leg while lunging forward.

2. Simultaneously, place your right arm on the floor for balance.

3. Keep your head looking forward.

4. Hold this position for 30 seconds, using your breath to explore if you can extend further forward comfortably.

5. Switch sides. If you initiated with your right foot and right arm, change to the left foot against the wall and left hand on the floor.

6. Hold for 30 seconds on the other side.

ARMS AND SHOULDERS

61. WALL SLIDE SHOULDER ELEVATIONS

Difficulty: Intermediate

Duration: 5 minutes

Repetitions: 3 sets x 10 reps

Instructions:

1. Stand facing the wall, arms at shoulder level, palms pressed against it.

2. Slide hands upward along the wall, keeping palms in contact.

3. Elevate shoulders towards ears.

4. Lower hands back down to the starting position.

62. SIDE WALL ARM STRETCH

Difficulty: Easy

Duration: 7 Minutes

Sets and Reps: 3 sets x 10 repetitions per side

Instructions:

1. Stand sideways to the wall, with the right side closer, maintaining feet shoulder-width apart.

2. Extend your arms forward at shoulder level, with palms facing each other.

3. Rotate your upper body to the left, moving the left arm outward towards the wall until the back of your left hand touches it.

4. Hold for a few moments, feeling the stretch along the left side.

5. Gently return to the initial stance and repeat on the other side.

63. WALL WALKS

Difficulty: Intermediate

Duration: 6 Minutes

Sets and Reps: 3 sets x 3 reps

Instructions:

1. Stand a few feet away from the wall, lean forward, and place palms on the floor.
2. Walk feet up the wall while moving hands closer, aiming for a handstand or near-vertical position.
3. Descend by walking hands away from the wall and lowering your feet.

64. WALL MOUNTAIN CLIMBERS

Difficulty: Intermediate

Duration: 5 Minutes

Sets and Reps: 4 sets x 45 seconds

Instructions:

1. Begin in a plank position facing away from the wall, with your hands below your shoulders.
2. Place your feet against the wall, creating an incline with the floor.
3. Engage your core and alternate pulling your knees toward your chest in a quick climbing motion.
4. Keep your spine straight and your core tight throughout.

65. HIGH WALL KNEE TUCKS (INVERTED)

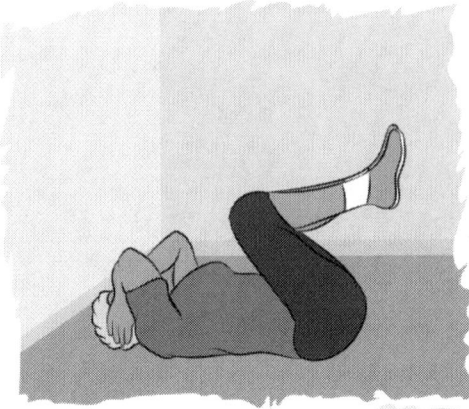

Difficulty: Intermediate

Duration: 6 Minutes

Sets and Reps: 3 sets x 15 reps

Instructions:

1. Stand close to the wall and raise your knees towards your chest.

2. Extend your legs without allowing them to touch the ground.

3. Maintain steady breathing throughout.

66. CHIN TUCKS AGAINST THE WALL

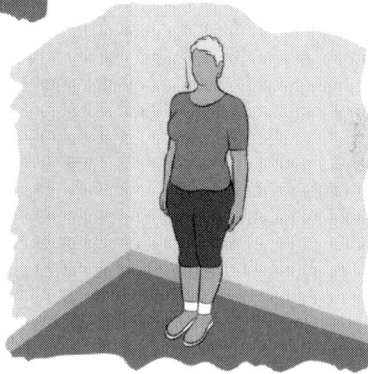

Difficulty: Easy

Duration: 4 Minutes

Sets and Reps: 3 sets x 10 repetitions

Instructions:

1. Stand upright with your back and heels against the wall, keeping your feet shoulder-width apart.
2. Stretch your spine and press the back of your head against the wall.
3. Draw your chin towards your chest, creating a double chin.
4. Maintain the tucked chin position briefly.
5. Relax and return to the initial position.

67. DIAMOND WALL PUSH-UPS

Difficulty: Beginner

Duration: 7 Minutes

Sets and Reps: 4 sets x 12 reps

Instructions:

1. Face the wall, arms stretched out, palms flat, forming a diamond shape with thumbs and index fingers.
2. Keep feet hip-width apart and engage the core.
3. Inhale, flex elbows, and bring the torso near the wall.
4. Exhale, and straighten arms to return to the initial stance.

68. WALL LATERAL RAISE SLIDES

Difficulty: Intermediate

Duration: 8 Minutes

Sets and Reps: 3 sets x 12 reps

Instructions:

1. Stand with your right side facing the wall, and extend your arm, with fingertips touching the wall.

2. Slide your hand up the wall, raising your arm.

3. Slowly slide your hand back down to the starting position.

4. Switch sides and repeat.

69. ARM CIRCLES WITH WALL RESISTANCE

Difficulty: Beginner

Sets/Reps: 2/15-20

Time: 3 Minutes

Instructions:

1. Stand facing the wall with arms extended at shoulder height.
2. Create resistance by pressing your palms into the wall.
3. Begin making small circles with your arms, gradually increasing the size.
4. Reverse the direction of the circles.
5. Perform 15-20 circles in each direction.

70. WALL PLANK ARM CIRCLES

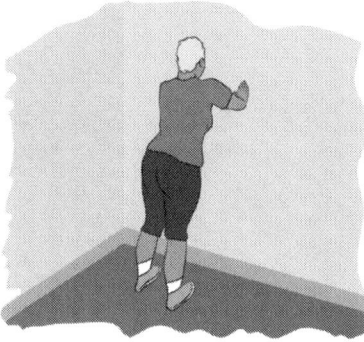

Difficulty: Intermediate

Duration: 8 Minutes

Sets and Reps: 3 sets x 8 reps (One rep includes circles in both directions for one arm)

Instructions:

1. Stand 2 feet away from the wall, with hands on the wall at shoulder level.

2. Lift one hand, make small clockwise circles for 8 counts, then counter-clockwise for 8 counts.

3. Switch to the other hand.

71. WALL-SUPPORTED SIDE PLANK WITH ARM RAISE

Difficulty: Intermediate

Duration: 8 Minutes

Sets and Duration: 4 sets x 15 seconds per side

Instructions:

1. Position on your right side with your feet against the wall, and rest on your right elbow.

2. Press your feet against the wall, extend your right arm, and raise your left arm.

3. Hold for 15 seconds, switch sides.

72. WALL CHEST OPENER

Difficulty: Intermediate

Sets and Reps: Not applicable

Instructions:

1. Stand sideways to the wall.
2. Extend the arm closest to the wall and press your palm against it.
3. Slowly rotate your body away from the wall, feeling a stretch across your chest and front shoulder.
4. Hold this stretch for 20-30 seconds before repeating on the opposite side.

73. WALL BUTTERFLY POSE

Difficulty: Easy

Duration: Hold for a few seconds

Instructions:

1. Sit on the floor with your buttocks positioned sideways to the wall.

2. Lean to either side, raising both legs against the wall.

3. Allow your legs to open gently, forming a triangular shape.

4. Bring your feet together, pressing them against each other.

5. Relax your arms to the floor or bring your hands into a prayer pose.

6. To exit, roll to either side and gently extend your legs.

74. WALL ANGELS

Difficulty: Easy

Duration: 5 Minutes

Sets and Reps: 3 sets x 10 repetitions

Instructions:

1. Stand with your back against the wall, making sure your feet are shoulder-width apart.

2. Slightly bend your knees for a neutral spine position.

3. Press the back of your head, upper back, and tailbone into the wall.

4. Arrange your arms in a "W" shape, with the back of your hands, forearms, and elbows against the wall.

5. Slide your arms upward into an "I" shape, maintaining contact with the wall.

6. Slowly slide your arms back down to the initial "W" position.

75. SHOULDER BLADE SQUEEZE

Difficulty: Easy

Duration: 5 Minutes

Sets and Reps: 3 sets x 15 repetitions

Instructions:

1. Stand near the wall, ensuring feet are shoulder-width apart and that your back firmly aligns with it.
2. Extend your arms forward at shoulder height, with palms facing each other.
3. Expand your arms to the sides, bringing the shoulder blades closer together.
4. Maintain for a few moments, sensing the involvement between your shoulder blades.
5. Return your arms to the initial position in front of you.

76. WALL ARM WINDMILL

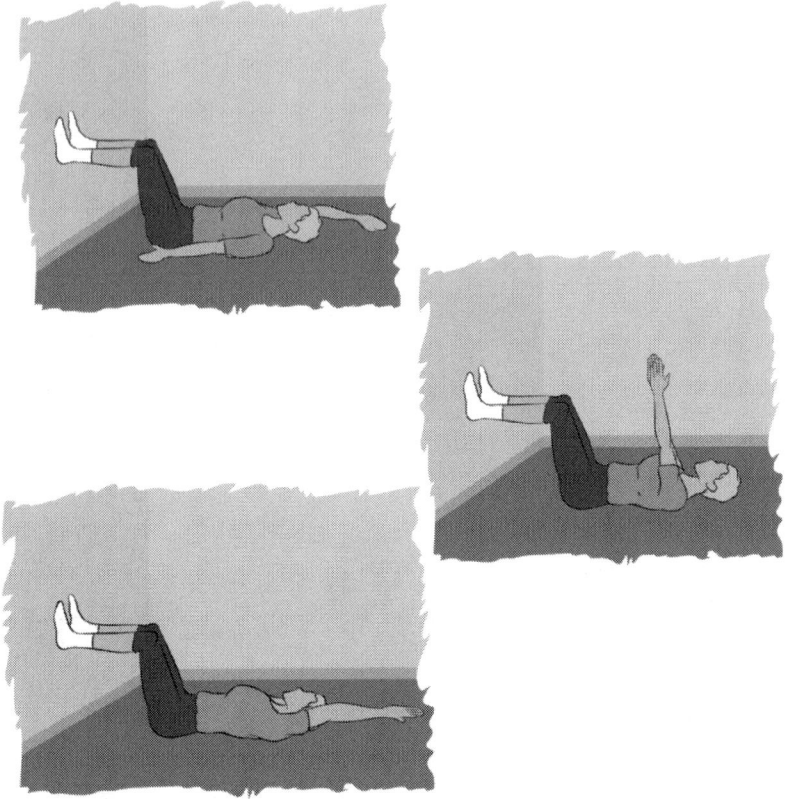

Difficulty: Beginner

Duration: Not specified

Sets and Reps: 10 repetitions

Instructions:

1. Lie on your back with one foot against the wall at a 45-degree angle. Elevate one arm upward on the floor and place the other firmly towards the wall.

2. Inhale, moving both arms towards the center simultaneously.

3. Exhale, release, and move your arms back to the floor, reversing the original arm positions.

4. Repeat for a total of 10 repetitions.

77. WALL TRICEPS DIPS

Difficulty: Easy to Moderate

Duration: Repeat 10 times

Instructions:

1. Stand facing a wall, a few feet out.
2. Place hands on the wall, slightly wider than shoulder-width.
3. Your body should align like the Wall Plank exercise.
4. Keep elbows tucked in, lower down until elbows press against the wall.
5. Push through palms, isolating strength from triceps to straighten arms and lift the body back up.
6. Repeat 10 times.

78. REVERSE WALL PLANK

Difficulty: Easy to Moderate

Duration: Hold for 15 seconds

Instructions:

1. Stand with your back facing the wall.

2. Keep elbows tucked in, lean back down until elbows press against the wall.

3. Your Body should form a straight line from head to heels, elbow holding against the wall at a comfortable angle.

4. Engage core and glutes, keeping weight on back heels.

5. Hold the position for a few breaths or as desired.

6. To exit, press into toes and stand up straight.

POSTURE EXERCISES

79. WALL SQUAT WITH CALF RAISE

Difficulty: Beginner

Duration: 8 Minutes

Sets and Reps: 3 sets x 15 reps

Instructions:

1. Stand parallel to a wall, 2 feet away, with your feet aligned with your shoulders.

2. Slide down the wall into a squat, then raise your heels off the ground.

3. Lower your heels to the ground and slide back up the wall.

80. WALL LEG RAISE TO BACK KICK

Difficulty: Intermediate

Sets/Reps: 3/12-15 (each leg)

Time: 4 Minutes

Instructions:

1. Stand facing the wall with your hands placed against it for support.
2. Lift your right leg straight to the side (leg raise).
3. Bring your right leg back down and kick it straight back (back kick).
4. Perform 12-15 leg raises to back kicks on each leg.

81. WALL PRESS AND CHEST STRETCH

Difficulty: Intermediate

Sets and Reps: 3 sets of 30 seconds

Instructions:

1. Stand approximately two feet (60cm) away from the wall, facing away from it.
2. Reach back and place your palms on the wall, fingers pointing upward.
3. Gradually increase the stretch by pushing your chest forward and bringing your shoulder blades closer together.

82. T-SPINE WALL STRETCH

Difficulty: Beginner

Duration: 5 Minutes

Sets and Reps: 4 sets x 40 seconds stretch

Instructions:

1. Stand, facing the wall, maintaining a distance of 1 foot, with feet shoulder-width apart.

2. Extend arms forward, placing palms against the wall.

3. Move hands upward on the wall, pivot at the hips, leaning towards the wall.

4. Ensure the head remains between the arms, intensifying the stretch in the upper back.

5. Take deep breaths to promote relaxation and release tension in the mid-back.

83. WALL STAFF POSE

Difficulty: Intermediate

Duration: Up to 30 seconds

Sets and Reps: Not specified

Instructions:

1. Lean your head and buttocks against the wall, with hands at the sides and toes directed upward.

2. Elongate your spine, and reach for maximum height without straining.

3. Stay in the position for up to 30 seconds.

84. WALL DOWNWARD FACING DOG

Difficulty: Moderate

Duration: 3 deep breaths per iteration

Reps and Set: Repeat 3 times

Instructions:

1. Stand facing a wall, approximately an arm's length away.

2. Place your hands comfortably on the wall above your head.

3. Slowly descend with your arms, bringing your head closer to the wall.

4. Press your chest towards the ground, ensuring your ears align with your upper arms.

5. Push your hips back, straighten your legs, and ground your heels.

6. Engage your core and sustain for 3 deep breaths.

7. Return to standing to release.

85. WALL PIKE

Difficulty: Moderate

Duration: Hold for 10-15 seconds

Instructions:

1. Start in a plank position with feet near the wall.

2. Walk feet up the wall, aligning hands under shoulders.

3. Press palms into the floor, spreading fingers wide.

4. Engage the core, move hands backward, and lift hips upward until directly over shoulders and head.

5. Keep head neutral between arms, gazing toward feet.

6. Hold the pose, breathing evenly.

7. Stay for 10-15 seconds.

8. To exit, carefully walk feet down the wall to return to the plank and stand up.

86. WALL SQUATS

Difficulty: Easy to Moderate

Duration: Hold for 10 to 60 seconds

Instructions:

1. Stand with your back against a wall, feet hip-width apart.

2. Slowly slide down the wall by bending your knees until your thighs are parallel to the ground or as far as comfortable, ensuring your knees are directly above your ankles, forming a 90-degree angle.

3. Hold the position for 10 to 60 seconds.

4. To exit, slide back up to the starting position.

LEG AND GLUTES EXERCISES

87. WALL CALF RAISES

Difficulty: Beginner

Duration: Repeat for 10 repetitions

Reps and Set: Repeat as desired

Instructions:

1. Stand facing a wall with feet hip-width apart and arms extended against the wall.

2. Inhale as you ascend onto the balls of your feet, raising your heels as high as possible.

3. Maintain for 2 seconds, then exhale and gradually lower heels back to the ground.

4. Repeat for 10 repetitions, ensuring calf engagement.

88. WALL LATERAL LUNGE

Difficulty: Intermediate

Duration: Perform 5 iterations per leg for a total of 10 reps

Reps and Set: 10 reps (5 per leg)

Instructions:

1. Place your hands on the wall and position your feet width apart.

2. With controlled movement, bend your right leg, guiding your body to the right. Keep the left leg as straight as possible.

3. Return to the center and repeat the lunge with the left leg.

4. Repeat 5 times on each leg for a total of 10 reps.

89. GLUTE BRIDGE WALL PRESS

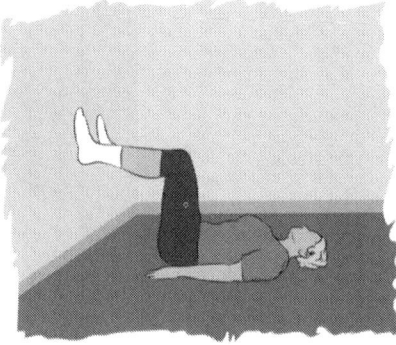

Difficulty: Intermediate

Duration: 5 minutes

Repetitions: 3 sets x 12 reps

Instructions:

1. Lie flat on a mat, feet against the wall at a 90-degree angle.
2. Arms along sides, palms down for stability.
3. Press feet into the wall, lift hips and engage glutes.
4. Press your feet harder for more engagement.
5. Lower hips down in a controlled motion.

90. ELEVATED WALL LUNGES

Difficulty: Intermediate

Duration: 8 Minutes

Sets and Reps: 4 sets x 10 lunges (5 per leg)

Instructions:

1. Stand 3 feet (90 cm) away from the wall, facing away, with your hands on your hips and feet hip-width apart.
2. Step forward with your right foot, ensuring the left foot's ball is against the wall at an angle.
3. Lower into a lunge, ensuring your right thigh is parallel to the ground.
4. Press down on your right heel to return to the initial position.
5. Repeat, alternating legs.

91. WALL SUPPORTED LEG SWINGS

Difficulty: Intermediate

Sets and Reps: 3 sets of 30 seconds for each leg

Instructions:

1. Stand sideways to the wall, using your hand for balance.
2. Swing the leg closest to the wall forward and backward, mimicking a pendulum motion.
3. After several swings, switch to swinging your leg side to side.
4. Perform each leg swing for 30 seconds before switching to the other leg.

92. WALL TWIST

Difficulty: Beginner

Duration: Repeat for 8 turns on each side

Reps and Set: 16 reps (8 turns each side)

Instructions:

1. Sit with your legs straight on the ground, optionally against the wall for balance.

2. Extend your arms at shoulder height and rotate your body to the right.

3. Exhale and pivot to the center, then turn your body to the left.

4. Repeat for 8 turns on each side for a comprehensive stretch of the arms and upper body.

93. THE SPINE STRETCH

Difficulty: Beginner

Duration: Execute for 3 repetitions

Reps and Set: Repeat as desired

Instructions:

1. Spread legs as far apart as feasible with the back against the wall.

2. Direct toes upward, with palms on each side of the floor.

3. Initiate stretching forward with each slide, reaching the maximum extent.

4. Upon reaching the limit, extend your arms as far as comfortable and sustain for 8 seconds.

5. Repeat for 3 repetitions, aiming to progress incrementally.

94. HIGH WALL GLUTE KICKBACKS

Difficulty: Intermediate

Duration: 8 Minutes

Sets and Kickbacks: 3 sets x 12 kickbacks (per leg)

Instructions:

1. Place the exercise mat perpendicular to a wall, toes a few inches away.
2. Start in a crawling position with forearms on the mat, forming a 45-degree angle with the wall.
3. Lift one leg, bend at the knee, and kick straight back.
4. Return the leg to the starting position.

95. KNEELING CHEST RAISE

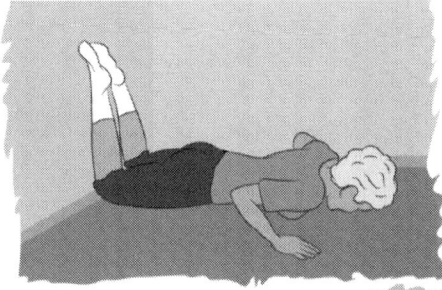

Difficulty: Beginner

Duration: Execute for 8 reps

Reps and Set: Repeat as desired

Instructions:

1. Begin supine with lower legs pressed against the wall, head facing downward.

2. Gradually ascend, elevating your chest and holding for 5 seconds.

3. Return to the starting position and repeat for 8 reps.

4. Sustain core engagement to prevent excessive back extension.

96. WIDE-LEGGED CHAIR POSE

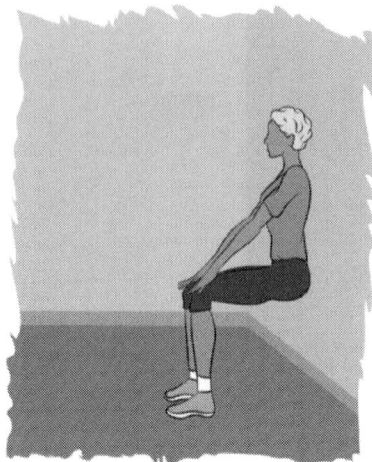

Difficulty: Easy to Moderate

Duration: Hold for up to 10 seconds

Instructions:

1. Stand with your back against the wall, feet wider than hip-width apart.

2. For an added challenge, turn your toes slightly outwards.

3. Engage your core, bend your knees, and slide down the wall until your thighs are parallel to the ground or as far as comfortable.

4. Ensure knees align with ankles and don't extend past your toes.

5. Extend arms in front, lifting them toward the sky.

6. Press your buttocks against the wall for stability.

7. Hold the pose, breathing deeply.

8. Stay for up to 10 seconds.

9. To exit, press through your feet and slide back up to standing.

97. GLUTE BRIDGE WALL SLIDES

Difficulty: Intermediate

Duration: 11 Minutes

Sets and Reps: 3 sets x 10 reps (for each leg)

Instructions:

1. Lie on your back with your feet against the wall, forming a 90-degree angle with your knees.

2. Lift your hips off the ground, engaging your glutes.

3. Slide one foot up the wall, then back down while maintaining the bridge position.

4. Repeat the movement with the other foot.

98. WALL SIDE LEG LIFTS

Difficulty: Intermediate

Duration: 8 Minutes

Sets and Reps: 3 sets x 12 reps (for each leg)

Instructions:

1. Stand 1 foot away from the wall, facing it with your right side, and have your right foot flat against the wall.
2. Lift your left leg to the side, engaging your outer thigh and glutes.
3. Lower the leg without allowing it to touch the floor.
4. Repeat the process on the other side.

99. ALTERNATING LEG SWINGS

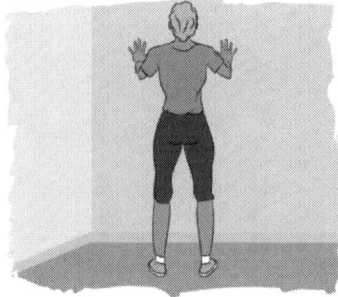

Difficulty: Beginner

Duration: Perform 20 swings (10 per leg)

Reps and Set: Repeat as desired

Instructions:

1. Stand upright facing the wall with arms extended against it.

2. Swing your right leg as far upward to the right as feasible, then gradually swing left.

3. Execute 10 full swings per leg for a total of 20 reps.

100. LEG CIRCLES

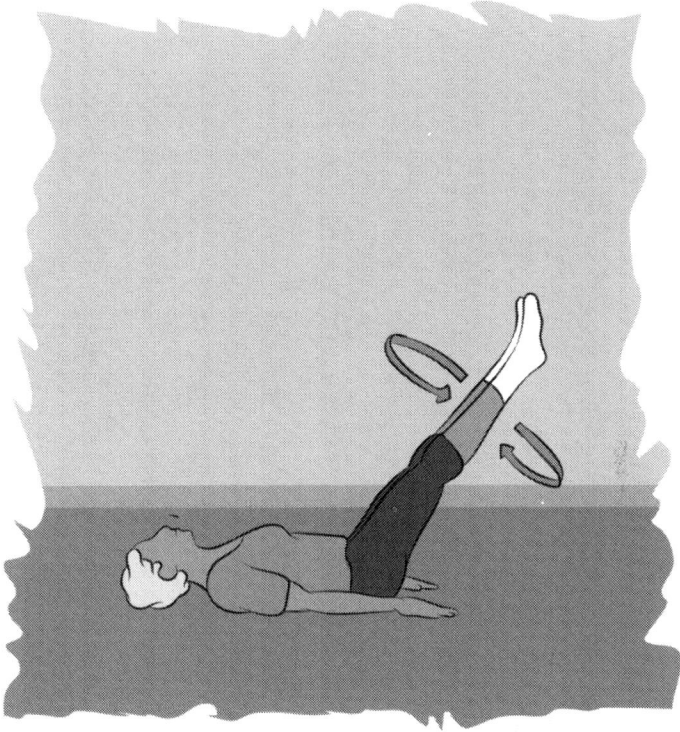

Difficulty: Easy to Moderate

Duration: 5 circles each leg (clockwise and counterclockwise)

Instructions:

1. Lie on your back, arms by sides, palms up.

2. Lift your legs toward the ceiling, and point your toes.

3. Circle the legs clockwise for 5 counts.

4. Switch to counterclockwise.

CONCLUSION

Earlier before you picked this book, you had a desire. It could be the desire to burn some calories and shed weight or a desire to stay in good shape and look younger than your age. Whatever your desire was, I am glad to see that you didn't just make the right choice of getting yourself a copy but also gave the effort and commitment to follow it through to this extent.

However, before you go show the world the new you, kindly take your time to explore the valuable recommendations, tips, and additional content on the remaining pages. With them, you get to supercharge your health and fitness pursuit.

You worked hard to come this far, and I am so proud of you!

UNDERSTANDING TUDCA AND ITS SIGNIFICANCE FOR HEALTH

TUDCA (tauroursodeoxycholic acid) is a distinctive bile acid naturally present in bile, albeit in small quantities. Its historical use in Chinese medicine spans millennia, primarily for aiding digestion and fostering liver wellness. Today, we can harness its benefits through supplementation.

TUDCA offers a plethora of advantages, including support for digestion, particularly in processing fats, as well as enhancing liver and kidney function, promoting brain health, bolstering cellular resilience, and maintaining eye health.

Endorsed by a multitude of medical professionals worldwide, TUDCA stands as a trusted recommendation for health and wellness, especially due to the fact that it is not sourced from the bile of any animal whatsoever.

TUDCA, despite being produced in minimal amounts within the human body, offers multiple benefits across various bodily functions, including:

1. Cognitive Enhancement: TUDCA's ability to traverse the blood-brain barrier positions it as a promising candidate for enhancing memory and cognitive abilities, making it a notable inclusion in the realm of nootropics.
2. Insulin Sensitivity Support: Studies indicate that TUDCA can mitigate cellular stress, potentially improving insulin sensitivity, which holds significance in conditions like diabetes.
3. Mitochondrial Function and Cellular Vitality: TUDCA's capacity to bolster mitochondrial health aids in enhancing energy production and combatting oxidative stress, thereby fostering cellular vigor and resilience.

4. Genetic Regulation: TUDCA's multifaceted impact extends to gene expression and DNA protection, exerting influence through mechanisms such as reducing oxidative damage and regulating cellular apoptosis.
5. Liver Wellness: Research demonstrates TUDCA's efficacy in promoting overall liver health by reducing liver enzymes and mitigating oxidative stress, though it does not reverse fatty liver disease.
6. Kidney Protection: TUDCA's ability to modulate inflammation responses contributes to supporting healthy kidney function amidst prevalent challenges such as mineral imbalances and dietary sodium excess.
7. Pathogen Defense: Studies highlight TUDCA's role in bolstering immune responses, particularly against certain viral infections, while its bile acid properties aid in combating unwanted pathogens in the digestive system.
8. Enhanced Bile Flow: TUDCA exhibits a remarkable capacity to significantly increase bile flow, which plays a pivotal role in digestion and nutrient absorption.
9. Gut Microbiome Support: TUDCA's influence extends to promoting a healthy gut microbiome by modulating inflammatory responses.
10. Eye Health Optimization: TUDCA shows promise in safeguarding against various eye-related issues and preserving the integrity of ocular cells.

In essence, TUDCA emerges as a multifaceted compound with far-reaching benefits for overall health and well-being, and also gains attention and credibility from both scientific communities and healthcare practitioners alike.

CASTOR OIL AND ITS AMAZING HEALTH BENEFITS

Castor Oil is an essential oil obtained from the Ricinus communis plant, which contains mainly Ricinoleic Acid and other constituents like Undecylenic acid, and Vitamin E.

Castor oil works like magic for hair growth, skin, liver, and lymphatic health. It helps to support lymph drainage and stimulates the bile duct, which is necessary to help improve our blood sugar, kill bacteria in the small intestine, and also emulsify fats.

Also, castor oil is very effective at oxygenating the body tissues, leading to improved circulation in the body, and helps the lymphatic system to seamlessly push wastes and germs out of our body systems.

Castor oil isn't just about improving circulation and the lymphatic system. Let me show you how it can boost your hair growth, reduce eye bags, glow your skin, and also keep your liver healthy.

FOR HAIR GROWTH OR DANDRUFF:

Instructions:

1. Get two or three tablespoons of castor oil, rub it on your hair, and ensure that it reaches your scalp.
2. If you are doing this before going to bed, wear a nightcap over your hair and let it work overnight till you wake up the next day.
3. Wash it off in the morning when you wake up.
4. If you are applying the oil outside bedtime, you can keep it in your hair for 20-60 minutes.

FOR EYEBROW GROWTH:

1. Using a cotton swab, rub a small amount of castor oil on your eyebrows.
2. Let it sit for twenty minutes or more.
3. Then wash it off when you reach your desired time.

FOR HEAVY EYE BAGS:

1. Massage the bags with castor oil to bring more tissue circulation to the affected area.
2. Alternatively, you can just place a castor oil pack on your liver gallbladder area to also enhance liver function.

FOR ACNE:

1. Just rub a little bit of castor oil on it, helping the lymphatic system drain wastes, bacteria, and toxins from the affected area.

Note: *Ensure to clean your face before use.*

FOR BETTER FACE COMPLEXION:

1. Mix one teaspoon of castor oil with an egg
2. Beat together to make a paste
3. Apply the paste on your face to form a face mask.
4. Then leave it on for a minimum of twenty minutes before washing off.

FOR SUNBURN:

1. Mix coconut oil and castor oil in equal proportions.
2. Mix them together and apply to your skin.

FOR CONSTIPATION/INDIGESTION:

1. Ingest one tablespoon of castor oil. This will go ahead to remove every blockage

Castor oil is a very effective and result-driven way to enhance your hair growth, improve your skin, and keep your internal organs working optimally.

NOTE: When getting your castor oil, ensure to get an organic one in a dark glass bottle.

28 DAYS WORKOUT PLAN

WEEK 1

DAY 1	DAY 2	DAY 3	DAY 4
Wall-Powered Plank Reach	Wall Handstand Leg Extensions	Wall Downward Dog	Glute Bridge Wall Press
Core-Strengthening Wall Squats	Wall-Supported Single-Leg Squats	Quad Stretch with Wall Support	Wall Squat with Calf Raise
Wall Dead Bug	Wall Push-Ups	Wall Cow Pose	Wall squats
Wall Plank with Back Kick	Wall Lateral Raise Slides	T-Spine Wall Stretch	Elevated Wall Luges

DAY 5	DAY 6	DAY 7
Isometric Wall Plank Hold	Light Stretching	Rest
Standing Wall Single-Leg Balance	Walking	
Wall Teaser		
Wall-Supported Tree Pose Stretch		

WEEK 2

DAY 8	DAY 9	DAY 10	DAY 11
Wall Hand-stand	Wall-Supported Pistol Squats	Wall Roll-Downs	Scapula Stretch
Wall Triceps Dips	Wall Leg Raise to Back Kick	Wall Side Leg Lifts	Wall-Supported Neck Stretches
Wall Chest Opener	Wall Split Progressions	ALTER-NATING LEG SWINGS	Happy Baby
Wall Arm Windmill	Wall Lateral Lunge	Wall Plank	Child's Pose

DAY 12	DAY 13	DAY 14
Wall Plank Arm Circles	Light Stretching	Rest
Wall Mountain Climbers	Walking	
Wall Shoulder Stand	Light Jogging	
Wall Downward Facing Dog		

WEEK 3

DAY 15	DAY 16	DAY 17	DAY 18
Wall-Supported Plank to Pike	Wall Press and Chest Stretch	Wall Dead Bug with Arm Slide	Wall-Supported Leg Swings
Wall Marches	Diamond Wall Push-Ups	Wall Leg Stretch	Wall Pike
Standing Side Bend Pose	Wall-Supported Side Plank with Arm Raise	Wall Calf Raises	Forward Fold Against Wall
Wall Bridge Extensions	Wall Angels	Wall Twist	Wall Staff Pose

DAY 19	DAY 20	DAY 21
Wall Roll Up	Walking	Rest
Wall Split Progressions	Jogging	
Wall Squat Holds		
Wall Twist		

WEEK 4

DAY 22	DAY 23	DAY 24	DAY 25
Isometric Wall Press	Wall Chest Opener	ALTER-NATING LEG SWINGSs	Wall Hundreds
Wall Plank with Back Kick	Reverse Wall Plank	Wall Supported Single-Leg Squats	Standing Wall Single-Leg Balance
Wall Downward Dog	Wall Triceps Dips	Wall Calf Raises	Wall Shoulder Stand
Wall Half Happy Baby Pose	Wall Handstand Leg Extensions	Wall-Supported Leg Swings	Wall-Assisted Half Body Plank

DAY 26	DAY 27	DAY 28
High Lunge Pose	Walking	Rest
Wall Downward Facing Dog		
Wall Handstand		
Wall-Supported Tree Pose Stretch		

BOOKS BY THIS AUTHOR

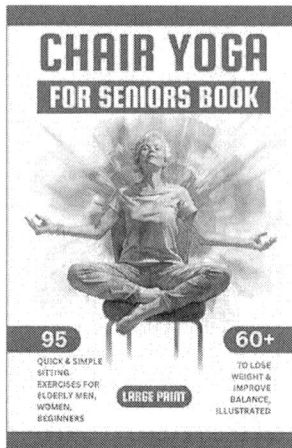

CHAIR YOGA FOR SENIORS BOOK
https://www.amazon.com/dp/B0CT6KP7CD

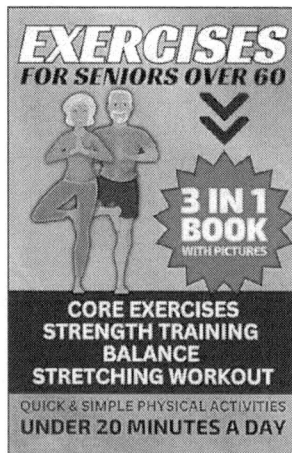

EXERCISES FOR SENIORS OVER 60
https://www.amazon.com/dp/B0CKB3YYBS

THANK YOU

Thanks for your purchase.

Having completed this book, we hope that you found it helpful in your pursuit of better health and overall wellness.

Kindly leave your feedback on this book on the product page as it will help spread the good news about it and inspire us to do more.

Thank you once again for your purchase.

21196744R10080